MOVING UP WITH SCIENCE
SOUND

Peter Riley

W
FRANKLIN WATTS
LONDON • SYDNEY

To my granddaughter, Holly Jane.

First published in 2015 by
Franklin Watts
338 Euston Road
London NW1 3BH

Franklin Watts Australia
Level 17/207 Kent Street
Sydney NSW 2000

HB ISBN: 978 1 4451 3520 5
Library ebook ISBN 978 1 4451 3521 2

Dewey classification number: 534

A CIP catalogue record for this book is available from the British Library.

Editor: Hayley Fairhead
Designer: Elaine Wilkinson

Photo acknowledgements: Aurinko p11b; Andy Crawford p6t, p12t, p12b, p14t, p14b, p16 all; Creativenature1 p15b; Himoreau1 cover main; Phillip Dyhr Hobbs p21; jstudio p19; Dmitry Kalinovsky p13m; Luchschen p8b; Ray Moller p6b, p7, p17, p18, p25; Nejron Photo p15t; Sashkin cover inset; Serrnovik p13b; Shutterbas p13t; Sjors737 p18b and p29; Tommaso79 title page and p24.

Artwork p12, p21: Proof Books
Artwork p7, p9, p15, p26: Ian Thompson
Artwork p11: John Alston

All other photographs by Leon Hargreaves.
With thanks to our models Sebastian Smith-Beatty, Layomi Obunabi and Sofia Bottomley.

Franklin Watts is a division of Hachette Children's Books, an Hachette UK company.
www.hachette.co.uk

Contents

Words in **bold** can be found in the glossary on pages 28–29.

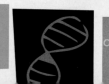

What's that sound?

What can you hear around you right now? Listen for one minute. Do the sounds change as you are listening? There are many kinds of sounds. One of the first things that scientists do when they study anything is group and **classify** what they are studying.

Classifying sounds

Sounds can be classified into loud and quiet sounds. A bus travelling down the road makes a loud sound. A purring cat makes a quiet sound. Another way to classify sounds is to group them into long and short sounds. The rumble of thunder makes a long sound. Plucking the strings on a guitar makes a short sound.

Shaking maracas makes a short sound.

Pitch

Sounds can have a **high pitch** or a **low pitch**. A teacher's whistle is a high-pitched sound. A dog growling is a low-pitched sound.

When you say the word 'ping' you make a high-pitched sound.

When you say 'toe' you make a low-pitched sound.

Make a table with these headings. Listen for sounds when you are out in the playground and tick the columns that describe each sound.

Sound	Loud	Quiet	Long	Short	High pitch	Low pitch
Children shouting	√		√		√	

How is sound made?

A sound is made when something **vibrates**. This means that it moves up and down or from side to side very quickly.

When the end of the ruler is released it moves up and down very quickly. It vibrates and makes a sound.

Vibration

A plastic ruler can be made to vibrate. Hold part of the ruler firmly on a tabletop and let the other part stick out over the table edge. Push the end of the ruler down a little and then release it quickly.

Sound waves

The vibrating tines on the tuning fork create small waves on the surface of the water.

You may wonder how the sound gets from the vibrating object to your ears. The following experiment gives a clue. When you strike a **tuning fork**, its tines (prongs), vibrate. If you dip the tines in water they make little waves across the surface of the water. When objects vibrate in air they make waves in the air.

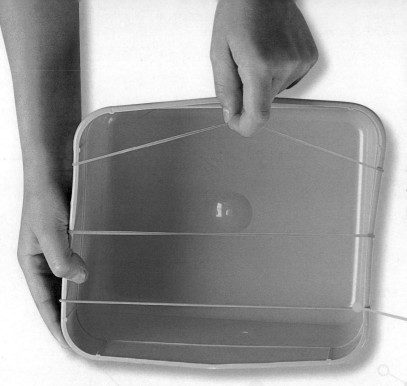

Movement of sound waves

Stretch an elastic band around a plastic box and pluck the band with your finger. The elastic band vibrates.

As the elastic band vibrates, the sound waves spread out in all directions.

vibrating elastic band

sound waves

Close your lips and blow through them so you make a sound like a motorbike. Can you feel your lips vibrate? Explain how the sound you are making reaches a friend's ears.

Seeing sounds

Our eyes normally cannot see sound waves, but certain scientific equipment lets us do just that.

Equipment for seeing sound

When sound waves reach a **microphone**, it changes them into tiny **currents** of electricity. These pass to an instrument that has a screen like a computer, which shows the sound wave shapes. This instrument is called an **oscilloscope**.

The tiny currents of electricity are displayed on the oscilloscope screen.

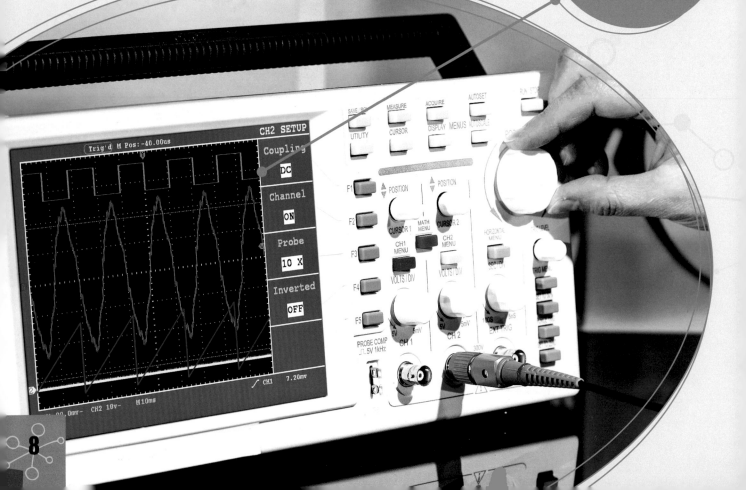

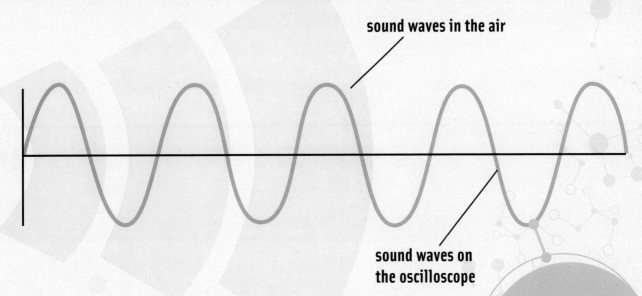

sound waves in the air

sound waves on
the oscilloscope

This picture shows how sounds make a wave pattern on the oscilloscope.

Parts of a sound wave

There are three parts to a wave. The **crest** is the top of the wave. The **trough** is the bottom of the wave. The **wavelength** is the distance from the start of the crest to the end of the trough.

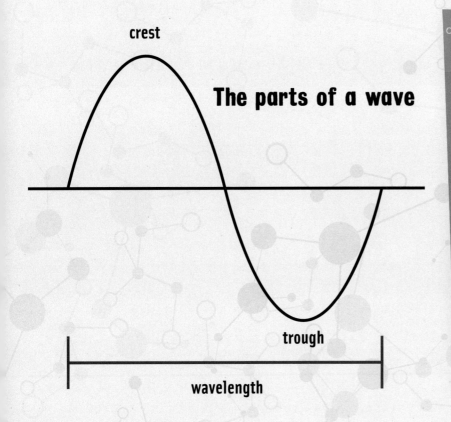

crest

The parts of a wave

trough

wavelength

Tie one end of a piece of rope to a fence or door handle. Stretch the rope, then let it sag. Shake the free end and look for a wave moving along the rope. What happens to the wave when you shake the rope slowly, quickly, gently or hard?

Sounds near and far

When something vibrates it sends out sound in all directions. If you are close to the vibrating object the sound is loud. But what happens when you move away?

When a drum is beaten the drum skin vibrates and makes a loud sound.

Distance from a sound

If you are close to a loud drum you may put your hands over your ears to block out the sound. When you begin to walk away, something happens to the sound you hear. The sound becomes quieter. As you walk further away, the sound becomes quieter still. Eventually, when the drum is far enough away in the distance, you cannot hear the sound it makes.

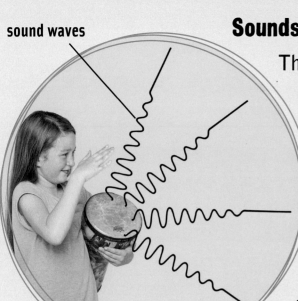

sound waves

Sounds and energy

This change in the loudness of the sound is due to **energy**. When you beat the drum, you use energy to hit it with your hand. The drum skin receives some of this energy and uses it to vibrate. The air receives some of the energy from the vibrating drum skin and waves are made in the air that spread out in all directions. As the waves move away from the drum they lose their energy, and become smaller and smaller until they stop.

These motorbikes are making a loud noise. What will happen when they move further down the road? Explain your answer.

Loud sounds, quiet sounds

SHOUT THESE WORDS to make a loud sound and whisper these words to make a quiet sound. You use a large amount of energy to make a loud sound and a small amount of energy to make a quiet sound.

quiet sound

loud sound

High and low sound waves

If you look at the waves of a loud sound on an oscilloscope you will see that they have high crests and deep troughs. This is due to the large amount of energy making the air vibrate strongly. The waves of a quiet sound have lower crests and shallower troughs than loud sounds. The smaller amount of energy makes the air vibrate less strongly.

The decibel scale

We measure length in centimetres (cm), temperature in degrees Celsius (°C) and sound in **decibels** (dB). We use the decibel scale to measure loudness. Here are some sounds on the decibel scale. Sound becomes painful to the ears at 130 dB and causes **permanent** damage to your ears at 160 dB.

Sound	Loudness (dB)
Jet aircraft taking off	130
Balloon popping	125
Road drill	110
Motorcycle	100
Lawn mower	90
Vacuum cleaner	80
A busy street	70
People talking	50
A quiet street	40
A whisper	30
In a library	20
Pin drop	10
Smallest audible sound (near total silence)	0

Use the table above as a guide to help you guess the loudness of the sounds in a busy town. Predict when you think the sounds will be the loudest and the quietest. Give reasons for your predictions.

Pitch

Say the words 'moo', 'mow', 'me', 'my'. You are making sounds of different pitch. 'Moo' is a low-pitched sound and 'my' is a high-pitched sound. The difference in the pitch of the sounds is due to the number of sound waves made every second. This number is called the **frequency** of the sound. Frequency is measured in units called **hertz** (Hz).

Slow and quick vibrations

Sound waves are made when something vibrates. If a long ruler is pressed down and released on the edge of a table, it vibrates quite slowly. If a short ruler is pressed down and released on the edge of a table, it vibrates very quickly.

The long length of the ruler makes a few waves in a second, so the sound has a low frequency. It has a low pitch.

The short length of the ruler makes many waves in a second, so the sound has a higher frequency and a higher pitch.

Low frequency

When sounds of different pitch are shown on an oscilloscope you can see the differences between the waves. Low-pitched, low frequency sounds produce a few waves every second on the oscilloscope screen. The waves have long wavelengths.

A growling lion makes a low-pitched, low frequency sound.

low frequency sound waves

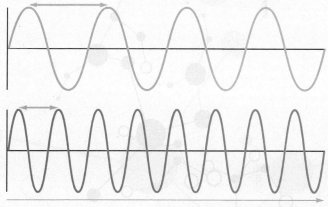

high frequency sound waves

A squeaking mouse makes a high-pitched, high frequency sound.

List the high- and low-pitched sounds you hear in a day. Which list is longer?

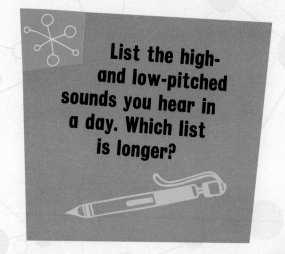

High frequency

High-pitched, high frequency sounds produce a large number of waves every second on the oscilloscope screen. The waves have short wavelengths.

Elastic bands and strings

Elastic bands and strings on musical instruments behave in similar ways. What you discover about a vibrating elastic band is the same for a vibrating string on a guitar or violin. Thinner elastic bands and strings make higher-pitched sounds than thicker elastic bands and strings when they are plucked.

When a thin elastic band is plucked it makes a higher-pitched sound than a thicker elastic band.

When a thick elastic band is held between finger and thumb and plucked, it makes a low-pitched sound.

If the same elastic band is stretched and plucked again, it makes a higher-pitched sound. Stretching an elastic band or string raises the pitch of the sound it makes.

Different lengths of string

A violin is a musical instrument with strings. It can be used to show another feature of a vibrating string. When the whole of the string is plucked, it vibrates and makes a low-pitched sound. If part of the string is held down to make a shorter length vibrate, it makes a higher-pitched sound.

The violinist presses down on the strings with one hand as she plucks with the other hand. The further her hand is from her face as she presses, the longer the string and the lower the pitch of the sound.

What happens to the pitch of a thick string on a musical instrument, such as a violin or guitar, when you tighten it up and then pluck it? What happens to the pitch when you loosen it again? How could you try and make a thick string vibrate at the same pitch as a thin string?

Wind instruments

When you blow into a wind instrument you make the air inside it vibrate. The vibrating air makes the sides of the instrument vibrate too, and the instrument makes a sound.

Brass instruments such as the trumpet are played by blowing a raspberry into them. You change notes by pressing valves and tightening your lips as you blow.

Long and short pipes

Think of a wind instrument as a pipe full of air. The length of the pipe affects the pitch of the sound it makes. A short pipe makes a high-pitched sound and a long pipe makes a low-pitched sound. Panpipes are made from wooden tubes of different lengths. They are arranged in order to make a **musical scale** when you blow across each of them in turn.

You make the air vibrate in a set of panpipes by blowing across their tops.

Changing the length of the pipe

A recorder is a tube with holes in it. You make the air vibrate in a recorder by blowing into a slot at one end. If you cover most of the holes with your fingers and thumb you make a long pipe. When you blow, you make a low-pitched **note**. If you lift some of your fingers to make a shorter pipe and blow again, you make a higher pitched note.

Covering different holes on the recorder makes different musical notes.

Blow across the top of an empty plastic bottle. Half fill it with water and blow again. What happens?

Speed of sound

How fast does sound move? Three hundred years ago William Derham measured the speed of sound using a clock and a cannon. He measured the time from seeing the cannon smoke to hearing it roar and calculated that sound travels at 348 metres per second. Today, more **accurate** experiments have shown that sound travels at 343 metres per second.

When sound waves reflect

Sound travels away from a sound source but what happens to it when it hits an object? You can test this question with an experiment. Hold a book in front of your mouth and say 'ahh' for as long as you can, whilst moving the book down away from your mouth and then back again. The sound waves are **reflected** off the book back to your ears.

The sound is louder with the book in front of your mouth because the sound waves reflect off the book.

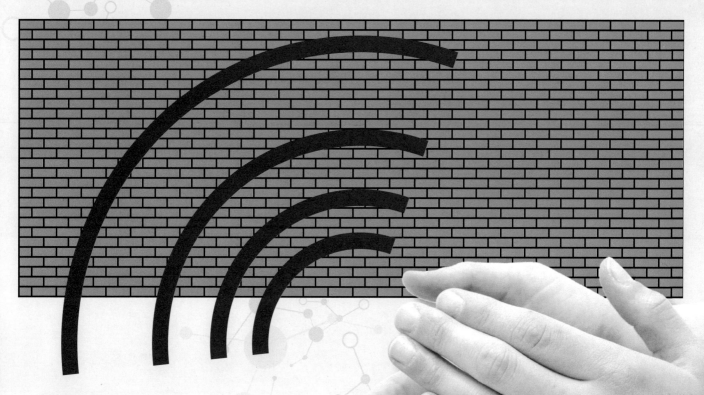

Echoes

For an ear to hear two sounds separately there needs to be at least a tenth of a second gap between the two sounds. If you stand just over 17 metres away from a high wall and clap your hands the reflected sound arrives over a tenth of a second later. You hear the reflected sound of you clapping as a separate sound called an **echo**.

What is the difference between William Derham's calculation and today's measurement of the speed of sound?

You can measure how fast sound travels by standing a measured distance (over 17 metres) from a wall and timing how long it takes from clapping to hearing the echo.

21

Sounds in solids and liquids

Sound travels through **gases** like the air around us, but does it travel through **solids**, such as wood, and **liquids**, such as water?

The table test

The movement of sound waves through a solid can be investigated in the following way.

1.
Bang a spoon on a table. You will hear the sound through the air.

2.
Bang a spoon on a table while pressing your ear to the tabletop. You will hear the sound through the solid part of the table. It is louder and clearer than the sound in air.

The balloon test

The movement of sound through a liquid can be investigated in the following way.

1.
Blow up a balloon until it is 10cm in **diameter**. Fill a second balloon with water until it is also 10cm in diameter.

2.
Place each balloon over a ticking watch in turn and place your ear gently on top of each balloon to listen for the sound. You can hear the sound of the watch more clearly through the balloon holding the water.

3.
Sound travels faster through liquids and solids than through air. The faster the speed of sound, the clearer the sound is to hear.

Look at the table opposite. How does the speed of sound vary in different materials? Can you explain why?

Material	Speed of sound (m/sec)
air	343
water	1500
steel	6000

Sound insulation

Loud sounds that go on for a long time can interfere with your concentration and your sleep. Very loud sounds can damage your ears and even make you deaf.

The ear protectors worn by this gardener prevent his ears from getting damaged by the loud machinery.

Covering your ears

A simple way to reduce a loud sound reaching your ears is to cover them with your hands. Loud sound waves have a lot of energy and have high crests and deep troughs. When they pass through your hands they use up energy and their crests fall and troughs rise. This makes the waves much quieter when they enter your ears. The **material** in ear protectors **absorbs** energy in the sound waves, making the waves smaller and quieter.

Covering the sound source

Loud sounds can be made quieter by wrapping the **sound source** in materials that absorb the energy in the sound waves as they pass through them. These materials are called sound insulation materials.

Finding the best sound insulator

You can find out how a material absorbs the energy in sound waves by:

1. Turning on a radio

2. Wrapping it in the material

3. Using your tape measure to find out how far you must move away until you cannot hear the radio.

You can use this method to compare materials and find which one is the best **sound insulator**.

Different materials absorb sound waves better than others. Paper makes a bad sound insulator, but foam makes a good sound insulator.

?

Where would it be useful to use sound insulators around your home?

Ears

We detect sound waves with our ears. What happens once these sound waves reach our ears? How do we hear?

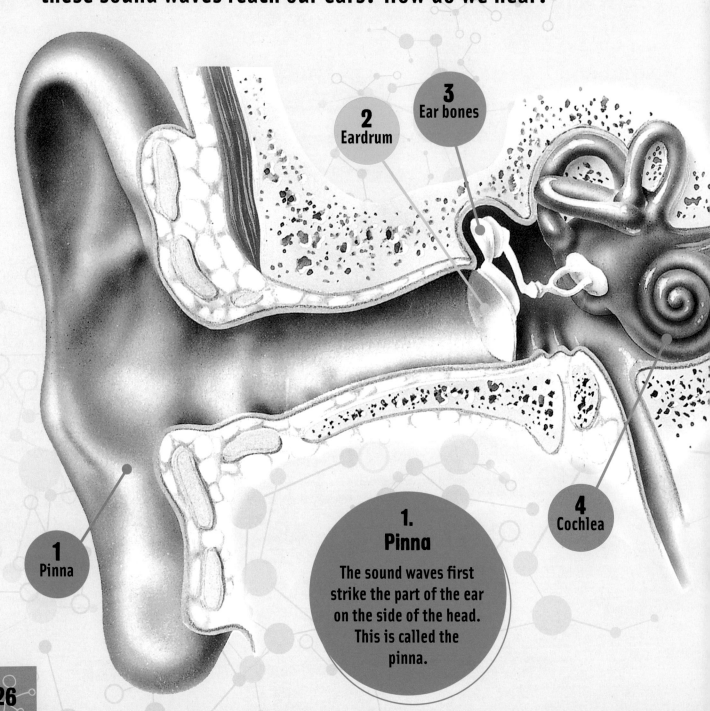

2 Eardrum

3 Ear bones

1 Pinna

4 Cochlea

1. Pinna

The sound waves first strike the part of the ear on the side of the head. This is called the pinna.

2.
Eardrum

The waves are reflected down a tube called the auditory canal. There is a very thin **membrane** stretched across the end of the canal. This is called the eardrum.

3.
Ear bones

When the sound waves strike the eardrum they make it vibrate. On the other side of the eardrum are three tiny ear bones. When the eardrum vibrates it makes the ear bones vibrate too.

4.
Cochlea

The cochlea looks like a snail shell. It has a little membrane in its wall called the oval window. When the ear bones vibrate the oval window vibrates too. The cochlea contains lots of tiny hairs and it is full of liquid. The vibrations pass through the liquid, which makes some of the hairs vibrate. They make nerves close by send electrical messages to the brain and we hear the sound.

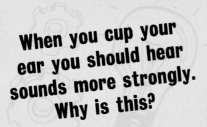

? When you cup your ear you should hear sounds more strongly. Why is this?

Glossary

Absorb to take in. A mop absorbs water. A sound insulator absorbs the energy in sound waves.

Accurate to be exact or correct when measuring.

Classify arrange things into groups to make them easier to study.

Crest the top of a wave, the mid-point between two wave troughs.

Currents (of electricity) the movement of tiny particles called electrons in wires and electrical equipment.

Decibel a unit for measuring the loudness of sound. The 'bel' part of the name is in honour of Alexander Graham Bell who invented the telephone.

Diameter the distance across a circle or circular object like a balloon.

Echo a reflected sound from a distant surface which sounds like the original sound.

Energy the power that waves use to go up and down and move outwards from a sound source.

Frequency the number of sound waves produced by a sound source in a certain time.

Gases materials which have no fixed shape or volume, but can flow and can be squashed.

Hertz unit for measuring frequency. It represents the number of waves produced per second. Humans can hear sounds from about 20 Hz (20 waves per second) to about 20 000 Hz (20 000 waves per second). The name is used in honour of scientist Heinrich Rudolf Hertz who discovered special waves called electromagnetic waves.

High pitch used to describe a sound like 'ping' which has a high frequency. The pitch of a sound depends on the frequency of the sound waves.

Liquids materials that have a fixed volume and cannot be squashed, but can flow and do not have a fixed shape.

Low pitch used to describe a sound like 'pong' which has a low frequency. The pitch of a sound depends on the frequency of the sound waves.

Material fabric or cloth.

Membrane a piece of material that is very thin, wide and flexible.

Microphone a piece of equipment that changes sound waves into electrical currents.

Musical scale a set of sounds called musical notes which increase or decrease in pitch as you play them. These sounds can be used to make music.

Note a sound made by a certain frequency of sound waves that is used for making music.

Oscilloscope a scientific instrument which changes sound waves to a wave picture on a screen.

Permanent to last forever and not change.

Reflected turned around and sent back in the opposite direction.

Solids materials that have a fixed shape and volume and cannot be squashed.

Sound insulator a material that absorbs a large amount of energy in sound waves and makes them quieter.

Sound source something that produces sound waves.

Trough the bottom of a wave, the mid-point between two wave crests.

Tuning fork a metal fork that produces a musical note when its tines vibrate. It is used for tuning instruments to make music.

Vibrate to move up and down or from side to side very, very quickly.

Wavelength the distance between the start of the crest to the end of the trough (which is the start of the next crest).

Answers to the activities and questions

Page 5 What's that sound?

Activity: Here are some examples:

Sound	Loud	Quiet	Long	Short	High pitch	Low pitch
Clock		✓		✓		✓
Doorbell	✓		✓			✓
Siren	✓		✓	✓	✓	
Motorcycle	✓		✓		✓	
Music	✓		✓	✓	✓	✓
Cat purring		✓	✓			✓

Page 7 How is sound made?

Activity: Lightly close your lips by touching your upper and lower front teeth and then gently blowing. The sound is like a 'putter, putter, putter'.

Your explanation could include the lips moving to and fro as they vibrate and making the air in front of them vibrate, sending sound waves through the air to your friend's ears.

Page 9 Seeing sounds

Answer: Shaking slowly produces a slow moving wave. Shaking quickly produces a faster moving wave. Shaking gently produces waves with low crests and troughs. Shaking harder produces waves with higher crests and deeper troughs.

Page 11 Sounds near and far

Answer: The sound will get quieter until the motorbikes can no longer be heard. When the motorbikes move into the distance the sound waves have to travel further and further. As they do so, the waves lose energy until they have none left to make crests and troughs.

Page 13 Loud sounds, quiet sounds

The loudness of the sounds will depend on the location of the listener. In town the sounds may be loudest when everyone is travelling to school and work. The quietest time in the town may be in the early morning when there is almost no traffic and nobody is on the streets.

Page 15 Pitch

Activity: The pitch of the sounds heard during a day will depend on the location of the listener at different times of the day. Someone who spends time on the computer in the evening may experience low-pitched sounds while someone who takes part in sport regularly may experience high-pitched sounds from whistles and sports shoes slipping on a gym floor.

Page 17 Elastic bands and strings

Answer: The pitch is high. The pitch is low. You tighten the thick string to make it vibrate at the same pitch as the thin string.

Page 19 Wind instruments

Activity: The pitch of the sound is raised when water is added to the bottle. This reduces the length of the wave vibrating in the bottle.

Page 21 Speed of sound

Answer: It was only five metres per second faster than the measurement made today.

Page 23 Sounds in solids and liquids

Answer: Sound waves move faster through water than through air, and faster again through steel. Sound travels faster through solids and liquids than through air.

Page 25 Sound insulation

Answer: The layers of glass in double-glazed windows can stop unwanted traffic noise disturbing you inside. Foam insulation can be put inside walls to stop noise travelling from one room to another.

Page 27 Ears

Answer: Your cupped hand makes a larger surface around your ear that can reflect sound waves into it.

Index

About this book

Moving Up with Science is designed to help children develop the following skills:

Science enquiry skills: researching using secondary sources, all pages; grouping and classifying, pages 5, 13, 15; observing over time pages 7, 9, 13, 21; comparative test pages 9, 13, 19, 27; pattern seeking page 13.

Working scientifically skills: making careful observations, pages 5, 9, 13, 15, 19, 21, 27; setting up a practical enquiry, pages 5, 9, 19 and 21; make comparative test, pages 5, 9, 13, 15, 19; using results to draw simple conclusions, page 13; using straightforward scientific evidence to answer questions, pages 7, 15, 19, 27.

Critical thinking skills: knowledge, all pages; comprehension pages 11, 23, 25, 27; application, page 17; analysis, page 21; evaluation, pages 13, 15.